The Roots of Rock and Roll

Scott Ingram and Tod Olson

SCHOLASTIC INC.

New York   Toronto   London   Auckland   Sydney
Mexico City   New Delhi   Hong Kong   Buenos Aires

Cover
© Michael Ochs Archives.com

Developed by ONO Books in cooperation with Scholastic Inc.

Copyright © 2003 by Scholastic Inc.
All rights reserved. Published by Scholastic Inc.
Printed in the U.S.A.

ISBN 0-439-59801-X

1 2 3 4 5 6 7 8 9 10   08   12 11 10 09 08 07 06 05 04 03

Contents

Welcome to This Book

What's your favorite kind of music? Rap? Metal? Hip Hop? Alternative? Punk? Pop? Whatever kind of popular music you listen to, chances are it started with rock and roll.

Rock and roll started out as a new sound in African-American nightclubs. Soon radio programs and concerts made it popular. Kids loved it. But their parents didn't. They thought the words were dirty. They thought the music was too loud. They thought it turned kids bad.

It sounds familiar, right? See how it all began.

Target Words

Here are some words that will help you understand the history of rock and roll.

- **integrated:** combining two different things, such as people of different races

  Rock and roll shows had integrated audiences.

- **morality:** people's idea of what is right and wrong or good and bad

  According to the morality of the day, rock and roll was dangerous.

- **obscene:** shocking in a way that's considered offensive

  Some people thought the words and heavy beat of rock and roll were obscene.

Reader Tips

Here's how to get the most out of this book.

- **Subheads** A subhead is like a title for a part of a chapter. It tells the main idea for that section. Look at the subhead on page 8. What do you think this section is about?

- **Read for Detail** Details are pieces of information about a topic. Look for information that answers the questions *who, what, where, when, why,* and *how.* These details will help you understand what you read.

1

Early Roots

Rhythm and blues was rocking in small nightclubs. But white people weren't listening.

What's that exciting new sound? It's coming from the Hideaway. That's a club in New Orleans, Louisiana. The South had already given birth to older musical styles such as blues and jazz. Now a new style of music called **rhythm and blues** (R&B) was catching on in African-American neighborhoods. And the Hideaway Club showcased the hottest music acts in town. In 1950, that was Fats Domino, sometimes known as the "The Fat Man."

Fats played the piano and sang upbeat party music. His left hand rolled up and down the keys. His right hand pounded high and fast. His songs had a beat that was hard to ignore. But not everyone was listening.

This is what many dance clubs looked like in the 1950s.

Dancing to Different Beats

In 1949, **segregation** was the law all across the South. Blacks were not allowed to use the same public bathrooms as whites. They weren't allowed to drink out of the same water fountains.

But even in the North, blacks and whites rarely socialized. They didn't live in the same neighborhoods. And for the most part, they listened to different music.

Most white people, young and old, listened to pop standards and folk music. Many of them weren't familiar with R&B music. Some had heard it but didn't like it very much. The beat was louder and stronger than what they were used to. Some of the lyrics were **suggestive.**

So when R&B first got started, artists like Fats played to all-black audiences. And they made records, too. But the records got limited play.

The big radio stations were aimed at white audiences. And most of them wouldn't play R&B. They called it "race music." In fact, *Billboard* magazine had separate lists, or charts, to keep track of the most popular records. There was "pop," "folk," and "race."

The white audience for pop and folk music was much larger. So, those musicians were getting rich. But R&B musicians like Fats Domino had a hard time supporting themselves.

"These cats could hardly make a living," said one band leader.

Little did people know that everything was about to change. Rhythm and blues was about to cross over to a new audience. And popular music would never be the same.

Heads Up!

Look up segregation *in the glossary. How did music reflect the way that society was segregated in the early 1950s?*

2

Bringing Down the House

The hall could hold 10,000 kids.
Twice as many showed up.

It was a rainy night on March 21, 1952, in Cleveland, Ohio. A huge crowd was gathering outside the Cleveland Arena. Everyone was there for the same reason. They wanted to hear some good R&B. It was no surprise that the majority of the crowd was African-American. But a handful of white kids showed up for the concert, too. And that was a surprise.

The man who planned the show was a local disc jockey named Alan Freed. But he was better known by his on-air nickname "Moondog." Freed was white, but he played race music. And young people loved it. So, Freed decided to hold a concert. He called it Moondog's Coronation Ball. The name of the concert gives you some idea of how Freed saw himself. A *coronation* is a ceremony to officially put someone on a throne. It seemed like Freed was hoping to create a new musical royalty.

Freed was amazed at how well tickets sold. Within a week, 7,000 were gone. Freed printed more, and they just kept selling. By the night of the concert, no one knew for sure how many tickets had been sold.

The Joint Was Jumping

When the doors opened that night, kids flooded in. At eight-thirty, the place was jammed, and thousands of people were still eager to get in. The police finally had to shut the doors.

The first act, Paul Williams and his band, came on stage. The lights went down, and they started playing R&B. The saxophones were honking and people were dancing.

---**Heads Up!**----------------

The police shut thousands of kids out of the concert. What do you think happened next?

MOONDOG CORONATION BALL
CLEVELAND ARENA
3717 EUCLID AVENUE — CLEVELAND, OHIO
FRIDAY NITE, MAR. 21
10 P.M. to 2 A.M.
IN PERSON FEATURING THESE SENSATIONAL STARS IN PERSON
PAUL WILLIAMS ★ TINY GRIMES
HUCKLEBUCKERS   ROCKIN' HIGHLANDERS
THE DOMINOES ★ DANNY COBB
MANY OTHERS! ★ VARETTA DILLARD ★ MANY OTHERS!
THE MOST TERRIBLE BALL OF THEM ALL! **THE MOONDOG RADIO SHOW** WITH **ALAN FREED** IN PERSON BROADCAST OVER WJW DIRECT FROM THE BALL THE MOST TERRIBLE BALL OF THEM ALL!
Adv. Sale Tickets $1.50 Including All Taxes Adm. at Door $1.75
TICKETS NOW ON SALE IN CLEVELAND AT RECORD RENDEZVOUS, 300 PROSPECT AND AT RICHMAN'S AND THE ARENA BOX OFFICE
ALSO AT MANY LEADING RECORD SHOPS IN OTHER NORTHERN OHIO CITIES

**DJ Alan Freed held the world's first rock and roll concert.
Radio ads and posters advertised the event.**

But fans who had been turned away burst in through the doors and windows. People were crushed against the stage. Fists flew and knife fights started. When a group of kids stormed the stage, the band stopped playing and ran.

The police finally regained control and sent the crowd home. The show was over almost before it started.

The city was shocked. *The Cleveland Press* complained about the young people rioting. And at least a few people blamed the music. An African-American newspaper blasted Freed's radio show. It said the music was dangerous. Freed's tunes spread bad taste and "low **morality**."

Freed said he was sorry. But inside, he was jumping for joy. The riot made him famous. He got more time for his radio show. And tapes of the show started playing in other cities. It wasn't long before more radio stations were playing music like Freed's. The audience for R&B music was starting to grow in size *and* color.

Heads Up!

How did the riot actually help Freed?

3

All Together Now

Rock and roll mixed things up.

Rhythm and blues was getting more popular. But now some people were calling it by another name: rock and roll.

Alan Freed was one of the first. He called his radio show "Moondog's Rock and Roll Party." The term came from African-American slang. It meant the same thing that "getting busy" means today. And it was used in many R&B songs, like "Good Rockin' Tonight" and "We're Gonna Rock, We're Gonna Roll."

Whatever you called it, one thing was clear. Teenagers couldn't get enough of this music.

In 1954, Freed decided to hold a Rock and Roll Ball in New York City. According to one of Freed's partners, Freed announced the concert only four times. Yet $38,000 came in the mail.

On January 14, 1955, the doors opened at New York's St. Nicholas Arena. Onstage were popular black musicians Fats Domino, Ruth Brown, Joe Turner, and more.

The white kids were thrilled. Many had tried to get into R&B shows before, but they had been turned away. Some clubs were afraid of trouble. It was a prejudiced time, and race mixing was considered **scandalous** in most places. And it was illegal in others.

Other clubs thought the risk was worth the extra profit. So, they sold tickets to whites, but they were extremely careful about it. The club might rope off a special section of the room. Whites were sold "spectator tickets." The white kids would have to stay inside the ropes. But at least they could hear the music. And they could try to copy how the black kids were dancing.

The Rock and Roll Ball was a different story. There, the young audience was **integrated.** No one could believe it. Black kids and white kids were all dancing to the same beat. They were dancing freely on the same dance floor. This had never happened before—not even in the North.

Salt and Pepper

Alan Freed knew he was onto something big. He threw other rock and roll parties and attracted even bigger crowds.

At first, the black performers couldn't believe what was happening. One of them was Chuck Berry, a singer, guitarist, and songwriter from St. Louis, Missouri. As a boy, Berry had learned to keep his distance from white people. So, when he saw crowds of white kids at Freed's shows, he was nervous. In fact, he said he found it "frightening." Where he was raised, it could be dangerous just to look a white person in the eye.

But after a while, Berry and the other black performers began to enjoy the change.

"Salt and pepper all mixed up together," Berry remembered later. "We'd say, 'Well, look what's happening.'"

Heads Up!

Chuck Berry said at first the change was "frightening." Why do you think he might have felt that way?

© Bettmann/Corbis

In 1955 Chuck Berry had his first big hit with "Maybellene."

Top of the Charts

Berry did more than watch his audience change. He helped it grow. He was one of the first musicians to write music he thought white kids as well as black kids would buy.

In 1955 Berry recorded a song called "Maybellene." The song didn't just make it to number 1 on Billboard's race chart. It hit number 5 on the pop chart, too.

Alan Freed played "Maybellene" all the time on his radio show. No one had ever heard anything like it, and today, some people say it was the first real rock and roll song.

The song was mostly rhythm and blues. The electric guitar chopped out a heavy, throbbing beat. But the song also had a bit of a country feel to it. In fact, it was taken from an old country fiddle tune. But the lyrics were about fast cars and young love.

This was a song that all young people could relate to. But most adults found it too loud and too fast. Rock and roll was becoming the music of teenagers.

Street Music

In the mid-1950s, some teens wanted to *make* music, not just listen to it. Many of these kids couldn't afford guitars or drums. All they had were their voices—and they decided to use them.

On street corners all around the country, teens met and started singing. They wrote their own tunes. Often they made up lyrics as they went along. Sometimes they just belted out sounds, like *ooh wah* or *shoobee doobee.*

Frankie Lymon was one of **doo-wop's** first big stars. Lymon grew up in Harlem. He got together with four friends: two were black, two were Puerto Rican. They called themselves The Teenagers. All of a sudden, they had a huge hit with "Why Do Fools Fall in Love."

Lymon rose from the streets to stardom when he was just thirteen. His success inspired thousands of kids to start singing. And doo-wop became the latest rock and roll craze.

About 30 years later, another craze was born on the same type of urban streets. During the 1980s, many young people began making music by chanting rhymes to strong beats. You may have heard of it. It's called rap.

Kids Against Adults

Does rock and roll turn kids into criminals?

In the spring of 1955, people flocked to see a new movie. It was called *Blackboard Jungle*. The film is about a crowd of tough city kids who basically take over a school.

"A drama of teenage terror!" the ads read. "They turned a school into a jungle!"

For most adults, the terror began with the film's **soundtrack.** As the film opens, the music of Bill Haley and the Comets blares through the movie speakers: "One, two, three o'clock, four o'clock, ROCK!"

In the movie, the students get into fights and refuse to listen to the adults. At one point, a teacher brings in some jazz records. The kids grab them and smash them against the wall. All the while, rock and roll music is wailing.

Kids Go Wild

Blackboard Jungle told adults what a lot of teenagers already knew. Teens had their own music, their own language, and their own way of doing things. And adults didn't get it.

Parents everywhere started worrying about their kids. Newspapers reported that teenage crime was on the rise. The U.S. **Congress** held **hearings** to figure out what was wrong.

Students at wealthy Princeton University were getting wild, too. One night in May, they started blaring "Rock Around the Clock" out their windows. Before long there was a party in the street. Students got out of control, setting fire to trash cans. The adults feared that even the"best and brightest" youth were being **corrupted.**

The media helped give rock its bad reputation. One TV announcer said that rock and roll was "as bad for kids as dope." In 1956, a story in *Newsweek* magazine reported that going to a rock and roll show was like entering another world. "An adult can actually be frightened," it said. *Time* magazine said a concert was like "the jungle birdhouse at the zoo."

These teens were in line for a rock and roll concert.
Some adults feared that rock and roll made teens go wild.

To many white adults, rock was still just "race music." And they didn't want their children to have any part in it. But they were only half right. "Rock Around the Clock" did come from an old R&B tune. But the singer, Bill Haley, was white.

In a few places, critics tried to protect their kids. Some radio stations refused to play rock and roll. Boston banned rock concerts for a while. Every now and then, police would show up at restaurants and nightclubs. They'd seize **jukeboxes** filled with rock records.

Bad Boys

For Alan Freed, the movie *Blackboard Jungle,* and the uproar that followed, had been great for business. The song "Rock Around the Clock" was a smash hit. Bill Haley and the Comets became the first white rock and roll stars. And Freed rushed to make a movie about the band.

Heads Up!

Why was rock and roll so disturbing to many adults? Give three reasons.

But Freed had seen what happened with *Blackboard Jungle*. And he didn't want his rock movie to be linked with violence. So, he made sure the musicians looked clean and safe.

Freed's movie *Rock Around the Clock* opened in April 1956. But despite Freed's efforts, some audiences got out of control. In Minneapolis and Hartford, teens came out of the movie and ran wild. In England, some kids threw lightbulbs from a balcony.

"We don't make boys bad!" Bill Haley told reporters during an interview.

But rock and roll already had a reputation.

Heads Up!

Name three ways in which adults tried to crack down on rock and roll.

5

Backlash

Rock and roll was bringing people together.
Some people didn't like it.

"Salt and pepper all mixed up together." That's how Chuck Berry had described the kids at rock and roll shows. It was definitely a sign that things were changing. Some people resented that.

In April 1956, the same month *Rock Around the Clock* opened, Nat King Cole played a concert in Birmingham, Alabama. Cole was famous for singing jazz and pop tunes in a silky smooth style. His music was nothing like rock and roll.

Soon after the show began, six white men rushed the stage. They attacked Cole, wrestled him to the ground, and beat him up. Afterward Cole brushed himself off and finished the concert. Then he vowed never to sing again in the South.

The whites who beat up Cole were members of a racist group called the White Citizens Council. After the attack, their leader, Asa Carter, spoke out against rock music. He said that it was "the basic, heavy-beat music" of Africa. He was sure that it was all part of a plot to mix the races.

Too Close for Comfort

Blues singer Ray Charles had an explanation for what was making some whites so angry.

"The young white girls run up and say, 'Oh, Nat!' And [white people] say, 'No, we can't have that!'"

"It was a time when many a mother ripped pictures of Fats Domino off her daughter's bedroom wall," said one music executive.

White anger bubbled up again when Frankie Lymon made a TV appearance. The teen doo-wop star appeared on a television show hosted by Alan Freed. Cameras showed him dancing with a white girl. Within days, angry phone calls and letters flooded the station. The show was canceled.

Around the same time, a crime commission in Houston came up with a list of thirty **obscene** songs. All were by black artists. A station in Memphis, Tennessee, banned another thirty musicians. All of them were black as well.

But white anger and laws could not stop what was happening. What had been considered race music was now all the rage with white teens. African-American slang was catching on in white suburbs. A "cat" was a cool guy. "Bread" meant money. "Crazy" meant cool or unusual.

Teens had spoken. And if their parents didn't like it, that was just too bad. Rock and roll was here to stay. And that was especially true because teens were speaking with their dollars. And the record companies heard them loud and clear.

—Heads Up!—

Reread the quote from Ray Charles. He doesn't directly say what the white people were afraid of. What was their fear?

You Go, Girls!

The first rock and roll stars were guys. But it didn't take long for girls to get into the act. In the late 1950s, all-girl singing groups started forming. By the early 1960s, record stores were full of songs by groups called the Poni-Tails, the Teddy Bears, the Crystals, and many more.

Most girl groups didn't write their own music. They performed songs written for them by professional songwriters. And they were backed by **studio** musicians.

But the girl groups did more than put a pretty face on rock and roll. They were the first to look at relationships from the female point of view. Classic songs include: "Soldier Boy," "He's So Fine," "He's a Rebel," "Mr. Postman," "It's My Party," and "My Boyfriend's Back."

Girl groups reached their **heyday** the sixties. Diana Ross and the Supremes were the most famous of them all. Like many of the girl groups, they had fancy matching outfits and choreographed routines.

Does that sound like any girl groups you know today?

Rock and roll may have started out as a "boy's club." But girl groups like the Crystals quickly got into the act.

6

Isn't That a Shame

Black music hit the charts.
But the faces were white.

In 1955, America met one of its most unlikely rock stars: Pat Boone. Boone was as clean-cut as they came. He had pretty-boy good looks. He wore white sweaters and white shoes on stage. He sang in a sweet voice that even a parent could love. And he was very religious.

Randy Wood is the man who discovered Boone. And according to Wood, Boone was just what rock and roll needed.

Wood was born and raised in the South. He owned a record store and a small recording company in Tennessee. In the early 1950s, he watched white teens come into his store and buy rhythm and blues records. This, he thought, could turn into big business.

Wood was convinced, though, that black artists would never make it big with whites. There was too much prejudice. So, to really make money, he needed white stars. He wanted them to sing rock and roll music. But he wanted a whitewashed version of it.

Pat Boone delivered just that. In 1955, Boone turned Fats Domino's "Ain't That a Shame" into a huge hit. But the bad grammar bothered Pat. So, when he introduced the song onstage, he called it "Isn't That a Shame." He also did a version of "Roll with Me, Henry." It was a song that blues singer Etta James had made famous. But straightlaced Pat called it "Dance with Me, Henry." When he did T-Bone Walker's "Stormy Monday," Pat changed the mention of wine to a soft drink.

Pat wasn't the only white musician **covering** black tunes. Bill Haley sang Fats Domino's "The Fat Man." Wood was right. The white versions sold millions more than the originals.

The reaction from black musicians was mixed. The music was theirs, and they usually got a cut of the profits for writing the song.

Pat Boone sang cleaned-up versions of R&B hits.

But most of the cash flowed straight past them into the hands of the white singers.

"With me there always had to be a copy," one of rock and roll's founding fathers, Bo Diddley, complained years later. "They wouldn't buy me, but they would buy a white copy of me. I don't even like to talk about it."

Eventually, many black artists were able to cash in once whites had made their songs famous. Fats Domino, for one, got a white audience after Boone and Haley did his songs.

Years after he covered "Ain't That a Shame," Pat Boone went to see Domino play in New Orleans. Fats called him up onstage.

"This man bought me this ring with this song," Fats said, pointing to a huge diamond ring.

The two performed "Ain't That a Shame." This time, Pat sang it as it had been written.

Heads Up!

White musicians recorded songs by African Americans. How did that help the African-American musicians? How did it hurt them?

7

The King Is Here

*Elvis brought rock and roll to TV.
And Americans were shocked.*

Sam Phillips ran a small record company in Memphis, Tennessee. He had a similar vision to Randy Wood's. "If I could find a white man who had the Negro sound, I could make a billion dollars," he would say to his secretary.

Unlike Wood, Phillips was looking for someone who sounded raw and real. He didn't want good grammar. He didn't want white shoes and a white sweater—just a white face.

In 1954, Phillips found his man. His name was Elvis Presley. Presley was a white truck driver from Memphis. He had sung gospel music in church. He had the sound.

In the summer of 1954, Phillips started sending Presley's tapes to radio stations. But he usually had trouble convincing people that Elvis was in fact a "white boy."

By 1956, Elvis was a huge hit, as Phillips had predicted. His single "Heartbreak Hotel" had hit the top of the charts.

Teens loved him. He wasn't a good boy like Pat Boone. He was tough. He wore his hair greased back on the sides and high on top. He kept his shirt collars turned up around his neck. At the time, that was really cool.

But what most people noticed about Elvis was the way he moved. He didn't just stand on stage and tap his feet to the beat. He swung his hips. He jiggled his legs. He curled his lip. And he danced with the microphone.

Young women went wild at the sight of Elvis. Their parents did too, but in a different way.

Hound Dog Music

On June 5, 1956 rock fans all around the country huddled in front of their televisions. Elvis was going on the popular "Milton Berle Show." Not many rock acts had been on TV. People tuned in by the thousands to check him out.

Elvis did a song called "Hound Dog." Halfway through, he slowed it down and hammed it up. He swung his hips wildly and hugged the microphone. The girls in the studio audience shrieked in delight.

The rest of the country cried out in shock. Most critics hated Elvis' music. "He can't sing a lick," wrote one. Another said he sang "in a whine." A congressman dismissed Elvis' sound as "hound dog" music.

But it was the dancing that bothered people the most. More than one writer compared Elvis to an animal. His movements onstage were all "grunt and groin," said one reviewer. They reminded him of a "mating dance."

Elvis was surprised and hurt by all the criticism. "When I sing this rock and roll, my eyes won't stay open and my legs won't stand still," he told a reporter. "I don't care what they say, it ain't nasty."

In July, Elvis went on TV again. He played "Hound Dog," but this time he toned it down.

The next day he went to the studio to record the song. A group of young fans met him with a protest. They carried signs that said, "We Want the Real Elvis."

They got it. Elvis recorded a rowdy version of "Hound Dog." And it went straight to the top of the charts.

Teenage America had spoken.

Heads Up!

Elvis' young fans protested for the "Real Elvis." And that's what they got. Why?

"When I sing this rock and roll," Elvis said, "my eyes won't stay open and my legs won't stand still."

Teens Rule

Before the 1950s, children and their parents generally enjoyed the same kinds of music, clothes, and movies. The idea of teen culture didn't exist as it does today. In fact, the word *teenager* didn't exist, either. (It was first used by *The New York Times* in 1945.)

But when World War II ended, things began to change. From 1946 to 1964, Americans had a record number of babies. Those kids started to hit their teen years in the late 1950s.

The post-war economy was good. Many teens had after-school jobs. By 1957, American teens had over $9 billion a year to spend.

Suddenly, teenagers were becoming powerful **consumers.** Companies began to market to them. Cars got bigger and faster. More movies about teen life, like *Blackboard Jungle,* were made. And rock and roll helped triple record sales between 1950 and 1959.

"Let's face it," said TV rock show host Dick Clark in 1958. "Rock and roll is the basic form of American popular music." And Americans had teenagers to thank for that.

8

Rock Gets Rich

Rock got down to business.

Rock and roll was becoming a different game. By 1960, big companies were in charge. These companies spent a lot of money to **promote** their stars. Nothing was left to chance. Huge profits were at stake.

Randy Wood and Sam Phillips created stars like Pat Boone and Elvis Presley. But that was only the beginning. Now, all record companies would control the look and sound of their stars. They would even try to control the radio airwaves.

This desire for complete control led to a big scandal in 1959. People found out that the record companies were slipping the DJs money, or **payola.** In return, the DJs played the record company's songs on the radio. The more play a song got on the radio, the better it sold.

On November 22, 1959, the scandal took down rock and roll's founding father. Alan Freed was fired by his radio station, WABC.

Freed had been the father of rock and roll. Ready to take his place stood a man named Dick Clark. Clark hosted a TV show called "American Bandstand." It was now the most popular show on daytime television.

The New Face of Rock

Like Freed, Clark played all the latest hits. But Clark's show didn't take risks. Rock stars didn't perform live. They lip-synched the words to taped music. Teens were filmed dancing to the music. But Clark's show had a strict dress code. Boys wore jackets and ties. Girls wore skirts and blouses.

"American Bandstand" also made it clear that there were limits to "salt and pepper mixing together." Only eight or nine African-American teens were allowed onstage at a time. Cameramen weren't allowed to focus on them for too long.

Rock and roll was making lots of money. It was being packaged and sold. But the product didn't turn out to be so easy to control, after all.

Jimi Hendrix is still considered one of the best rock and roll guitar players who ever lived.

Epilogue

During the 1960s, a new sound was coming out of Detroit, Michigan. A small, black-owned recording studio called Motown had a sound all its own. It came to be known as "soul music." And that grew into a new sound called "funk," which later led to disco.

In the late 1960s, rock and roll got political. At that time many young people were protesting the Vietnam war. Protest music didn't get much play on **corporate** stations. So, FM radio was born. Suddenly, rock was wild again.

Artists explored all kinds of sounds: music from India, old-time country music, and more. A great guitarist named Jimi Hendrix experimented with feedback noise. He changed the sound of rock. And he became a rock-and-roll idol to a largely white audience.

Concerts like Woodstock showed how popular this underground music was. So, it wasn't long before the big companies found a way to profit. They bought up the FM stations. For a while, it seemed like rock was back under control.

Then in the late 1970s, angry young kids started to rebel against "corporate rock." They decided to take music into their own hands. They didn't know how to play, but they blasted out a style that was angry and loud. That kind of music became known as punk. Punks invented their own rock-and-roll fashion to go with their music.

But punks weren't the only ones getting creative. In the early 1980s, young kids in the inner city created their own form of music, too. Many couldn't afford to buy instruments and expensive equipment, so they **improvised.** They scratched records on old turntables to get a beat. They made up rhymes and held contests to see whose were the best. That was the birth of rap.

Today, you can hear everything from punk to rap, and music that is a blend of both. And why not? After all, these musical styles all share the same roots — the roots of rock and roll.

—Heads Up!—

How much do you think your friends know about the roots of rock and roll?

Glossary

Congress *(noun)* the body of the United States government that makes laws (p. 21)

consumer *(noun)* someone who buys and uses products (p. 39)

corrupt *(verb)* to make someone bad (p. 21)

corporate *(adjective)* having to do with large companies called corporations (p. 43)

cover *(verb)* to play your own version of someone else's song (p. 31)

doo-wop *(noun)* a rock and roll singing style that uses a harmony of voices (p. 19)

hearing *(noun)* a meeting called by politicians to gather information about something (p. 21)

heyday *(noun)* a time when something was at its greatest or most popular (p. 28)

improvise *(verb)* to make something up as you go along (p. 44)

integrated *(adjective)* combining two different things, such as people of different races (p.15)

jukebox *(noun)* a machine that plays records (now CDs) when money is placed in it (p. 23)

morality *(noun)* people's idea of what is right and wrong or good and bad (p. 13)

obscene *(adjective)* shocking in a way that's considered offensive (p. 26)

payola *(noun)* money record companies paid to disc jockeys for playing records (p. 40)

promote *(verb)* to advertise (p. 40)

rhythm *(noun)* the beat of a song (p. 6)

rhythm and blues (R&B) *(noun)* blues-based music with a strong beat (p. 6)

scandalous *(adjective)* immoral and shocking to people (p. 15)

segregation *(noun)* the practice of keeping black people and white people apart (p. 8)

soundtrack *(noun)* the music that goes with a movie (p. 20)

studio *(noun)* a place where musicians make records (p. 28)

suggestive *(adjective)* suggesting something considered improper (p. 8)

Index